# High-Protein Plant Based Cookbook

Tasty Vegan Recipes for a Strong, Vital and Healthy Body, How to Increase Your Energy and Strenght Without Affecting the Natural Environment

Written By

**JANE BRACE**

# Table of Contents

BUTTERY SHORTBREAD 85

CHOCOLATE SHORTBREAD 87

SPECULOOS 89

SPECULOOS BUTTER 91

PIZZELLES 92

SNOW CAP COOKIES 94

TUXEDO SANDWICH COOKIES 96

COCONUT CARAMEL COOKIES 98

LEMON SANDWICH COOKIES 101

ROLLED GINGERBREAD COOKIES 103

FIGGY FILLED COOKIES 105

SPRINGERLES 108

CINNAMON GRAHAM CRACKERS 110

RUGELACH 112

CRISPY GLAZED LIME COOKIES 114

PALMIERS 116

LAVENDER ICEBOX COOKIES 117

MOCHA CRUNCHERS 119

MATCHA COOKIES 121

LADYFINGERS 123

MADELEINES 125

# TOPPINGS: FROSTINGS, GLAZES, AND SAUCES

# MARSHMALLOW FONDANT

**YIELD: COVERS ONE 2-LAYER CAKE**

Fondant is one of those wonderful things that can help transform a cake from "meh" to "marvelous!" It is easy to use and can be made into multiple colors. You can also use fondant to make cute cut out shapes to paste onto your cake. Once you've covered your cake, roll out a thin layer and then cut out using cookie cutter—see Rolling Fondant. Lightly brush one side with water and paste it to the cake.

1 bag (10 ounces) vegan marshmallows, such as Dandies

¼ cup warm water

1 teaspoon vanilla extract (optional)

½ tablespoon refined coconut oil, plus ¼ cup for kneading and greasing

2 to 3 drops food coloring (optional)

1½ cups confectioner's sugar + about ½ cup extra for kneading

- Thoroughly grease a silicone spatula and mixing bowl.

- Place the marshmallows into a medium saucepan and heat over medium-low heat until sticky, for about 5 minutes, stirring often. Add the water, vanilla extract, ½ tablespoon coconut oil, and food coloring, if desired. Continue to cook over medium-low heat until completely smooth, for about 7 minutes, stirring often with the greased silicone spatula.

- Transfer to a very well greased mixing bowl. Carefully beat in 1½ cups confectioner's sugar until tacky. There most likely will be confectioner's sugar remaining in the bottom of the bowl. It's okay, just leave it.

- Using greased hands, remove from the bowl and knead in about ½ tablespoon coconut oil and more confectioner's sugar until the dough is no longer sticky. It should take quite a few small additions of confectioner's sugar, about ½ cup total, to get it to the right consistency.

- Wrap in plastic wrap and chill overnight. Remove the fondant from the refrigerator about 10 to 15 minutes before using. Store in airtight container in refrigerator for up to 2 weeks.

# Rolling Fondant

Whether you use my recipe for Marshmallow Fondant, or opt for store-bought, such as Satin Ice brand, working with fondant is easier than it looks; in fact, I think it's the easiest way to make a spectacular-looking cake with little fuss. You simply need to have a few inexpensive tools on hand to make it look flawless.

Always keep a small container of coconut oil handy for greasing your hands as fondant tends to dry out quickly but can easily be saved by massaging a touch of coconut oil or shortening into it.

When working with fondant, I recommend having a few special tools on hand to make the experience easier. A fondant roller and rubber rolling rings are handy, as well as a fondant spatula, which will enable a smooth application onto your cake.

The most important tip I can offer is to make sure that the cake you are covering is even. Use a serrated knife to carve the cakes into even layers (usually only the very top needs to be trimmed) and fill in gaps with a little extra frosting. Use the method on to create a crumb coat, and, if desired, add a final layer of frosting to the outside of the cake. Now you are ready to cover the cake.

When rolling out fondant, be sure to roll out onto a very clean, flat, and lightly confectioner's sugared surface. Use plastic rings on a fondant roller to determine the thickness of your fondant, which will ensure an even layer on your cake. Use the fondant roller to help lift the rolled fondant and transfer it evenly onto the cake. Mend any tears or cracks with a touch of water and/or coconut oil. Finally, smooth out the cake with the fondant spatula, gently moving the spatula over the fondant in a circular motion to remove any large bumps or bubbles. You can insert a clean pin into any small bubbles to "pop" them before smoothing over, if needed. Seal edges with fondant balls or piped icing.

# BUTTERCREAM FROSTING

**YIELD: 4 CUPS**

A standard in any dessert lover's arsenal, this recipe works exceptionally well with either margarine or coconut oil. If you opt for the latter, add a pinch of salt and keep slightly chilled.

6 tablespoons non dairy margarine or coconut oil (cold)

6 cups confectioners sugar

2 to 3 teaspoons vanilla extract

6 tablespoons non dairy milk

2 additional tablespoons softened non dairy margarine or coconut oil

- Cream together the 6 tablespoons margarine and about ½ cup of the confectioner's sugar. Gradually add in other ingredients, except the softened margarine. Once all the other ingredients have been combined and are fairly smooth, add in softened margarine.

- Mix on very high speed, using a whisk attachment, whipping until fluffy.

- Use immediately on cake, or chill in fridge for later use. If refrigerated, make sure you let it soften slightly by setting the icing out at room temperature just until it is softened enough to spread easily onto cake. If you find the icing too thick, add a touch more nondairy milk to thin. Store in airtight container in refrigerator for up to 2 weeks.

# FLUFFY BAKERY-STYLE FROSTING

**YIELD: 2 CUPS**

Use this classic frosting to fill Whoopie Pies, cupcakes, and more. This frosting can easily be made up to 1 week ahead of time and stored in the refrigerator before using. Be sure to thaw to room temperature before using.

2 cups confectioners sugar

1 cup non hydrogenated shortening

¼ cup non dairy margarine

- Beat together the ingredients in an electric mixing bowl, or by hand, until fluffy. Store refrigerated and allow to warm slightly at room temperature before piping or spreading onto cakes or cookies. Store in airtight container in refrigerator for up to 1 week.

# CREAM CHEESE FROSTING

**YIELD: 1¼ CUPS**

A foolproof recipe with a tangy twist. Feel free to sub in 1 cup Sweet Cashew Cream + 1 teaspoon lemon juice in place of the vegan cream cheese. To make a drizzly glaze rather than a fluffy frosting, simply thin with 2 to 3 tablespoons nondairy milk and 1 teaspoon agave or corn syrup.

8 ounces nondairy cream cheese

2 cups confectioners sugar

* Make the icing by mixing the ingredients vigorously by hand, or using an electric mixer, until fluffy. Chill before using. Store in airtight container in refrigerator for up to 1 week.

# FLUFFY CHOCOLATE FROSTING

**YIELD: 2 CUPS**

Better than the stuff from a can, but just as addictive. Top your favorite cupcakes or use as a filling in between cookies, like the Vanilla Wafers.

⅔ cup cocoa powder

⅓ cup non hydrogenated shortening

¼ cup softened non dairy margarine

¼ cup non dairy milk

2½ cups confectioner's sugar

* In a large mixing bowl fitted with a whisk attachment, combine the cocoa powder, shortening, and margarine until smooth. Gradually add the non dairy milk and confectioners sugar and then beat on high speed until fluffy, scraping down the sides as needed. Makes enough for one sheet cake; double recipe if making for a layer cake. Store in airtight container in refrigerator for up to 2 weeks.

# GERMAN CHOCOLATE ICING

**YIELD: TOPS 1 GERMAN CHOCOLATE CAKE**

This sweet coconutty icing makes an apropos topper for German Chocolate Cake, but it's just as scrumptious in other applications as well! Try it atop a big scoop of Vanilla Soft Serve.

½ cup agave

¾ cup powdered sugar

2 tablespoons non dairy milk

1 cup pecans, finely chopped

2 tablespoons coconut oil, softened

2 cups sweetened shredded coconut

* In a medium bowl, whisk together the agave, powdered sugar, and nondairy milk until smooth. Add the rest of the ingredients and mix well. Spread onto cakes while they are still warm, or pipe onto cupcakes using a bag with no tip. Store in airtight container in refrigerator for up to 2 weeks.

# CARAMEL FROSTING

**YIELD: COVERS 12 CUPCAKES**

This rich and velvety frosting is reminiscent of sweet and salty caramel candies, without the need to slave over the stove. Even though this frosting goes stunningly with the recommended Bourbon Caramel Cupcakes, this also tastes fantastic on chocolate cake. For an over-the-top treat, try it slathered on top of my Ultimate Fudgy Brownies, and sprinkled with toasted pecans.

2 cups confectioners sugar

½ teaspoon vanilla extract

1 tablespoon molasses

¼ cup non dairy milk

⅛ teaspoon salt

1 tablespoon non dairy margarine

- Combine all ingredients, in the order given, into a small electric mixing bowl and mix on high speed until smooth and tacky. Spread generously onto the tops of cooled cupcakes or layer cake. Store in airtight container in refrigerator for up to 2 weeks.

# MOCHA-FLUFF FROSTING

**YIELD: 1½ CUPS**

This frosting is best used right after preparing, since as it cools, it hardens into a fantastically light and airy, candy-like topping.

1 cup vegan marshmallows, such as Dandies

1 tablespoon non dairy margarine

2 teaspoons instant espresso powder

2 cups confectioners sugar

1 tablespoon non dairy milk

- In a small saucepan, heat the marshmallows, margarine, and espresso powder over medium-low heat until the marshmallows and margarine have melted. Stir constantly and then immediately transfer into a mixing bowl equipped with a whisk attachment. Blend on low as you add in the sugar and nondairy milk and then increase speed to high and whip just until fluffy. Quickly transfer into a piping bag fitted with a large round tip and pipe onto cupcakes.

You can double the batch of this recipe and make a confection a lot like a vegan meringue. Just pipe onto parchment or waxed paper and let air-dry for about 6 hours.

# VANILLA GLAZE

**YIELD: 1 CUP**

Particularly nice for glazing one-half of a Black and White Cookie, this glaze also works well for cakes, Blondies, and pretty much any treat you can think of.

1 cup confectioners sugar

1 tablespoon + 1 to 2 teaspoons non dairy milk

1½ teaspoons light corn syrup

⅛ teaspoon vanilla extract Dash salt

- In a small bowl, whisk all the ingredients together until very smooth, ensuring no lumps remain. Use immediately after making and let set for at least 1 hour before handling.

# CHOCOLATE GLAZE

**YIELD: 1 CUP**

This super-easy glaze tastes just like the icing on popular chocolate snack cakes and makes a perfect alternate glaze for Petits Fours.

⅓ cup melted non dairy chocolate coins or chips

1 teaspoon coconut oil

⅓ cup confectioners sugar

1 teaspoon corn syrup

1 tablespoon non dairy milk

* In a small bowl, whisk together the chocolate and coconut oil until smooth. Gradually add the confectioner's sugar, corn syrup, and nondairy milk, stirring continuously to blend. Stir vigorously until very smooth. Use immediately to top cookies and cakes. Let set for 2 hours before handling.

# LEMON GLAZE

**YIELD: 1 CUP**

Perfect atop Lemon Cake or drizzled onto Sugar Cookies, this glaze sets
quickly and should be prepared right before using.

1 large lemon, sliced thinly

1 cup sugar

1½ to 2 cups confectioners sugar

1 teaspoon corn syrup

* In a 2-quart saucepan over medium heat, bring the lemon slices and sugar to
  a gentle boil and let cook for 1 minute. Remove from heat and strain the
  liquid into a medium bowl. Mix in the confectioner's sugar and corn syrup
  until smooth and creamy. Drizzle onto cooled cakes or cookies and let rest
  for 1 hour before serving.

# ROYAL ICING

**YIELD: 2 CUPS**

This icing has numerous uses, from piping intricate decorations on cookies, to gluing gingerbread houses together. Make this icing right before using for easiest application. For best results, use a piping bag equipped with a small round tip.

2 cups confectioners sugar

3 tablespoons non dairy milk

1 tablespoon corn syrup

* Place all ingredients into a medium bowl and whisk together until very smooth. Use immediately.

# RAINBOW SPRINKLES

**YIELD: 2 CUPS**

DIY sprinkles for cakes and cookies are very simple, and it gives you the option to make your own sprinkles using all-natural food dyes.

1 recipe <u>Royal Icing</u>

4 or 5 different colors of food coloring, paste, or drops

- Prepare the Royal Icing according to recipe directions and divide evenly among four or five small mixing bowls. Place 1 or 2 drops of each color into the individual bowls until the desired colors are achieved. Place one color of icing into a piping bag fitted with a very small round tip (or you can use a plastic storage bag with just the tip of one corner cut off). Pipe a long skinny stream of icing onto a silicone mat or sheet of waxed paper. Repeat with all colors and let dry completely. Once dried, use a sharp knife to cut into small jimmies.

# DARK CHOCOLATE GANACHE

**YIELD: 2 CUPS**

This delicious cake topper couldn't be easier to make, and it only contains two ingredients. Use the best-quality chocolate you can get your hands on for exceptional flavor. Ganache makes a lovely filling in between cakes and cookies, too, especially the Vanilla Wafers.

¾ cup full-fat coconut milk

1½ cups non dairy chocolate chips

- Heat the coconut milk in a small saucepan over medium heat just until it begins to bubble. Remove from heat. Place chocolate chips in small bowl and then stir in hot coconut milk to melt the chips. Let cool until slightly thickened.

# DEVILISHLY DARK CHOCOLATE SAUCE

**YIELD: 1 CUP**

Espresso and cocoa powders combine for a sinfully rich sauce. Easy to make, it is great served warm over ice cream, or drizzled onto cheesecakes for an extra-special touch.

⅔ cup dark cocoa powder

½ teaspoon espresso powder

1⅔ cups sugar

1¼ cups water

1½ teaspoons vanilla extract

* In a medium saucepan, whisk together the cocoa powder, espresso powder, sugar, and water. Over medium heat, bring the mixture to a boil and let cook for 1 minute, while stirring constantly. Remove from heat and stir in vanilla extract. Let cool before transferring to an airtight container. Store in refrigerator for up to 2 weeks and reheat to serve warm or use cold.

# HOT FUDGE SAUCE

**YIELD: 1½ CUPS**

Better than the kind you can buy from the store, this hot fudge sauce keeps for up to 1 month if stored in an airtight container in the fridge.

1 cup sugar

⅓ cup cocoa powder

2 tablespoons brown rice flour (superfine is best)

2 tablespoons coconut oil

1 cup non dairy milk

1 teaspoon vanilla extract

* In a small saucepan, whisk together all of the ingredients and heat over medium heat. Continue to stir as the mixture heats, ensuring no lumps remain as the mixture gets hot. Reduce the temperature slightly and continue to cook until thickened, for about 3 to 4 minutes. Stir well right before serving and enjoy hot.

* Store in airtight container in the refrigerator for up to 1 month, and reheat as needed to top ice cream and other goodies.

# BUTTERSCOTCH SAUCE

**YIELD: 2 CUPS**

Salty and sweet butterscotch sauce was always my favorite topper for ice cream. I like having a jar stowed away in the fridge for those inevitable ice cream sundae cravings.

¼ cup non dairy margarine

1 cup packed brown sugar

¾ cup canned full-fat coconut milk

½ teaspoon vanilla extract

- Place the margarine into a 2-quart saucepan over medium heat and melt slightly. Add in the brown sugar and heat until the margarine and sugar have mostly melted.

- Once liquefied, add the coconut milk and vanilla extract and stir well. Continue to cook over medium heat for 9 minutes, stirring often. Turn off heat and let cool slightly. Whisk together well and transfer to a glass jar. Let cool completely before capping and transferring to the refrigerator. This will keep for up to 3 weeks.

# CARAMEL SAUCE

**YIELD: 1 CUP**

This easy caramel sauce was created for topping the Caramel Chai Cheesecake but is also incredible over ice cream, especially with sprinkles.

1 cup brown sugar, packed

½ cup non dairy margarine

¼ cup almond or coconut milk

1¼ teaspoons vanilla extract

* In a 2-quart saucepan, whisk together the ingredients and warm over medium heat. Cook, stirring, just until the mixture has thickened to a creamy caramel sauce consistency, for about 5 minutes. Store in airtight container in refrigerator for up to 2 weeks.

# CAPTIVATING COOKIES AND BARS

*Who doesn't love* a cookie? They come in all shapes, sizes, textures, flavors, and colors, are easy to prepare, and are always a crowd-pleaser—especially when they are free of a few common allergens, like dairy, eggs, and gluten!

You may want to invest in a few cookie jars to house all these cookies and bars. If the baking bug hits you hard, cookies do make wonderful gifts.

# DROP COOKIES

# CLASSIC CHOCOLATE CHIP COOKIES

**YIELD: 24 COOKIES**

Crispy, chewy, and crunchy, these chocolate chippers are just like the ones the corner cookie shop makes. Be sure to let these rest for at least 30 minutes before transferring from cookie sheet.

2 tablespoons flaxseed meal

4 tablespoons water

1 cup non dairy margarine

1 cup sugar

1 cup packed brown sugar

1 teaspoon vanilla extract

1 teaspoon baking soda

2 teaspoons warm water

2 cups sorghum flour

1 cup brown rice flour

½ cup tapioca flour

1 teaspoon xanthan gum

1 cup semi-sweet non dairy chocolate chips

- Preheat oven to 375°F.

- In a small bowl, mix the flaxseed meal with the water and allow it to rest for at least 5 minutes, or until thick. Cream together the margarine and sugars until smooth. Add in the vanilla extract and prepared flaxseed meal. Blend together the baking soda and water and add into the creamed margarine mixture.

- In a separate bowl, whisk together the rest of the ingredients up to the chocolate chips. Gradually stir the flours into the margarine mixture until a clumpy dough forms. It should be doughy, but not sticky. If it is too sticky, you will need to add more sorghum flour, about 1 tablespoon at a time, until it becomes a soft dough.

- Shape the dough into rounded spoonfuls and place onto an ungreased cookie sheet about 2 inches apart. Bake on the middle rack about 11 minutes, or until slightly golden brown on edges.

- Store in airtight container up to 1 week.

# OATMEAL RAISIN COOKIES

**YIELD: 24 COOKIES**

Addictively easy, these are always a welcome addition to a standard cookie tray. If you're like I was as a kid, feel free to sub in chocolate chips for the raisins.

2 tablespoons flaxseed meal

¼ cup water

1 cup non dairy margarine

1 cup brown sugar

1 teaspoon vanilla extract

1 cup brown rice flour

½ cup potato starch

¼ cup tapioca flour

1 teaspoon xanthan gum

1 teaspoon baking powder

3 cups certified gluten-free oats

1 cup raisins

- Preheat oven to 350°F. In a small bowl, combine the flaxseed meal with the water and let rest for 5 minutes, until gelled.

- In a large mixing bowl, cream together the margarine and sugar until smooth. Add in the vanilla extract and the prepared flaxseed.

- In a medium bowl, whisk together the brown rice flour, potato starch, tapioca flour, xanthan gum, and baking powder. Stir into the creamed sugar mixture. Fold in the oats and raisins.

- Shape the dough into about 1½-inch balls and place onto an ungreased cookie sheet about 2 inches apart. Flatten slightly and bake on middle rack for 15 minutes. Let cool completely before serving. Store in airtight container for up to 1 week.

# PRETENTIOUSLY PERFECT PEANUT BUTTER COOKIES

**YIELD: 24 COOKIES**

To be able to call oneself "perfect" takes a good bit of gusto, but man oh man, do these cookies deliver! Chewy, but crunchy, and baked until gloriously golden, these can also be perfect almond, cashew, or sunflower butter cookies if you have a peanut allergy. Simply swap in another nut or seed butter.

½ cup non dairy margarine

¾ cup smooth peanut butter

½ cup sugar

½ cup packed light brown sugar

1 tablespoon flaxseed meal

2 tablespoons water

¾ cup sorghum flour

¼ cup tapioca flour

½ cup potato starch

¾ teaspoon xanthan gum

¾ teaspoon baking soda

- Preheat oven to 375°F.

- In a large mixing bowl, cream together the margarine, peanut butter, and

39

sugars until smooth. In a small bowl, mix the flaxseed meal with the water and allow it to rest for at least 5 minutes, or until thick. Add into the peanut butter mixture.

- In a separate bowl, whisk together the rest of the ingredients and then gradually incorporate into the peanut butter mixture until all has been added and a clumpy dough forms. Roll dough into 1-inch balls and flatten the cookies using a fork, forming a crisscross pattern and pressing down gently but firmly. Place 2 inches apart onto an ungreased cookie sheet.

- Bake for 11 minutes. Remove from the oven but let remain on cookie sheet until completely cooled. Store in airtight container for up to 2 weeks. These also freeze nicely.

# SNICKERDOODLES

**YIELD: 24 COOKIES**

Some speculate that Snickerdoodles have German roots, while others believe that the name "Snickerdoodle" was just another whimsical cookie name made in the nineteenth-century New England tradition. Regardless of the source of the name, these cookies are another childhood favorite.

2 tablespoons flaxseed meal

4 tablespoons water

½ cup non dairy margarine

½ cup non hydrogenated shortening

1½ cups sugar, plus 4 tablespoons for rolling

1 teaspoon vanilla extract

2 teaspoons cream of tartar

2 teaspoons baking soda

½ teaspoon salt

1 cup sorghum flour

1 cup millet flour

¾ cup potato starch

1 teaspoon xanthan gum

1 tablespoon cinnamon, for rolling

- Preheat oven to 375°F.

- In a small bowl, mix the flaxseed meal with the water and allow it to rest for at least 5 minutes, or until thick.

- Cream together the margarine, shortening, and 1½ cups sugar until smooth. Mix in the prepared flaxseed meal, vanilla extract, cream of tartar, baking soda, and salt.

- In a separate bowl, combine sorghum flour, millet flour, potato starch, and xanthan gum. Slowly combine the flour mixture with the sugar mixture and mix vigorously (or use an electric mixer set on medium-low speed) until a stiff dough forms.

- In another small bowl combine the 4 tablespoons sugar with the cinnamon.

- Roll dough into 1-inch balls and then roll each dough-ball into the cinnamon sugar mixture.

- Place 2 inches apart on an ungreased cookie sheet and bake for 9 minutes.

- Remove from oven, sprinkle with a touch more sugar, and let cool on cookie sheet for about 5 minutes.

- Transfer the cookies to a wire rack and let cool for at least 20 more minutes before handling. Store in airtight container for up to 1 week.

These tender cinnamon sugar–speckled cookies need a lot of space when baking. Be sure to place them at least 2 inches apart on a cookie sheet or the cookies will merge together.

# TRAIL MIX COOKIES

**YIELD: 24 COOKIES**

These cookies feature all my favorite flavors of trail mix baked right into a scrumptious cookie. The options for mix-ins are endless. Try pepitas, dried blueberries, or even your favorite spice blend to shake things up!

½ cup smooth peanut butter

½ cup non dairy margarine

1½ cups turbinado sugar

1 teaspoon vanilla extract

3 tablespoons flaxseed meal

6 tablespoons water

¼ teaspoon salt

1 cup sorghum flour

½ cup brown rice flour

¼ cup almond meal

½ cup potato starch

¼ cup tapioca flour

1 teaspoon xanthan gum

1 teaspoon baking powder

½ cup shredded coconut (sweetened)

1 cup non dairy chocolate chips

½ cup sliced almonds

½ cup raisins

- Preheat oven to 375°F. In a large bowl, cream together the peanut butter, margarine, sugar, and vanilla extract until smooth. In a small bowl, mix the flaxseed meal with the water and allow it to rest for at least 5 minutes, or until thick. Add in the prepared flaxseed meal.

- In a separate bowl, whisk together the salt, sorghum flour, brown rice flour, almond meal, potato starch, tapioca flour, xanthan gum, and baking powder. Gradually add the flour mixture into the peanut butter mixture and mix until a dough forms.

- Fold in the coconut, chocolate chips, almonds, and raisins until incorporated.

- Drop by rounded tablespoonfuls onto an ungreased cookie sheet 2 inches apart. Flatten slightly with the back of a spoon and bake for 12 minutes, or until bottoms are golden brown. Let cool completely on the rack before enjoying. Store in airtight container for up to 1 week.

If you use a sugar other than turbinado, you may need to add 1 to 2 tablespoons of nondairy milk to get a proper dough to form.

# SUPER-SOFT CHOCOLATE CHIP
# PUMPKIN COOKIES

**YIELD: 20 COOKIES**

Just as the name implies, these cookies are super soft and chock-full of pumpkin goodness. I love making these for Halloween parties, as they are always quick to get gobbled up!

½ cup non dairy margarine

1⅓ cups sugar

1¼ cups canned (or fresh, drained well in cheesecloth) pumpkin puree

1 teaspoon vanilla extract

1 teaspoon baking powder

½ teaspoon baking soda

1 teaspoon sea salt

1¼ cups sorghum flour

¾ cup brown rice flour

½ cup potato starch

¼ cup tapioca flour

1 teaspoon xanthan gum

1 cup non dairy chocolate chips

- Preheat oven to 350°F.

- Cream together the margarine and sugar. Once smooth, mix in the pumpkin.

- In separate bowl, mix together the rest of the ingredients except for the chocolate chips. Slowly fold the flour mixture into the pumpkin mixture just until mixed. Fold in the chocolate chips.

- Drop by tablespoonfuls onto an ungreased cookie sheet about 2 inches apart. Bake for 17 minutes. Remove from oven and let cool completely before enjoying. Store in airtight container for up to 1 week.

If using fresh pumpkin with these, be sure to strain the pump kin very well so that very little liquid remains before adding to the cookies.

# GARAM MASALA COOKIES

**YIELD: 18 COOKIES**

If you think garam masala is only good for savory dishes, these cookies will open your eyes! With warming notes of brown sugar, vanilla, and the delicious Indian spice blend, what's not to love?

1 cup cold non dairy margarine

¾ cup sugar

¾ cup brown sugar

1 teaspoon vanilla extract

2 teaspoons baking powder

2 teaspoons garam masala

1 teaspoon xanthan gum

2 tablespoons apple cider vinegar

¼ cup almond flour

1 cup buckwheat flour

½ cup sweet white rice flour

2 tablespoons cocoa powder, for dusting

- Preheat oven to 375°F. Cream together the margarine and sugars. Add the vanilla extract, baking powder, garam masala, and xanthan gum. Add the vinegar and then gradually mix in all of the flours a little at a time until well blended.

- Using a tablespoon, scoop out round balls onto an ungreased cookie sheet about 3 inches apart. Bake for about 10 minutes, or until the cookies have flattened out completely.

- While they are still warm, sprinkle a touch of cocoa powder on each cookie. Store in airtight container for up to 1 week.

# MAPLE COOKIES

**YIELD: 24 COOKIES**

Crispy on the inside and cakey in the middle, these irresistible cookies will have you reaching in the cookie jar again and again with their seductive maple flavor. For an extra-indulgent treat, top with the glaze from Mini Maple Donuts.

1 tablespoon flaxseed meal

2 tablespoons water

½ cup non dairy margarine

½ cup brown sugar

½ cup maple syrup

1 teaspoon maple extract

1 teaspoon baking soda

1¾ cups superfine brown rice flour

1 cup potato starch

¼ cup cornstarch

¼ cup tapioca flour

1 teaspoon xanthan gum

½ teaspoon salt

½ cup turbinado sugar

* Preheat oven to 350°F. Line a cookie sheet with parchment paper. Mix the flaxseed meal with the water in a very small bowl. Let rest for 5 minutes, or

until gelled.

- In a large mixing bowl, cream together the margarine, sugar, and maple syrup until fluffy. Mix in the prepared flaxseed meal and maple extract.

- In a medium bowl, whisk together the remaining ingredients, except for the turbinado sugar, and then gradually incorporate into the creamed margarine until a soft dough is formed. Do not overmix.

- Form into 1-inch balls and roll in the turbinado. Flatten slightly with the back of a fork and bake for 15 minutes, rotating the cookie tray after 10 minutes' baking time. Let cool completely before removing from cookie sheet. Store in airtight container up to 1 week.

# PECAN SANDIES

**YIELD: 24 COOKIES**

Be sure to serve with a tall cold glass of almond or rice milk!

1 tablespoon flaxseed meal

2 tablespoons water

½ cup non dairy margarine

½ cup olive oil

½ cup confectioners sugar

½ cup sugar

1¼ cups brown rice flour

½ cup potato starch

¼ cup tapioca flour

1 teaspoon xanthan gum

½ teaspoon baking soda

½ teaspoon cream of tartar

½ teaspoon salt

1 cup chopped pecans, plus 24 whole pecans for topping

- Preheat oven to 375°F.

- Mix the flaxseed meal with the water in a very small bowl. Let rest for 5 minutes, or until gelled. In a large bowl, mix together the margarine, oil, sugars, and prepared flaxseed meal until blended.

- In a separate bowl, whisk together the brown rice flour, potato starch, tapioca flour, xanthan gum, baking soda, cream of tartar, and salt. Add the flour mixture to the sugar mixture and stir well to combine into a slightly oily dough. Add the chopped pecans.

- Form into 1-inch balls, place 2 inches apart onto an ungreased cookie sheet, and place a single pecan on top of each cookie. Bake for 11 minutes, or until lightly golden on the edges.

- Let cool completely before serving. Store in airtight container for up to 1 week.

# COCOA MACAROONS

**YIELD: 24 COOKIES**

These simple cookies are ooey, gooey, and chewy with a crispy crunchy outer shell. Perfect for snacking. If you want to change it up a bit, try the Australian method and place a small bit of jam or a fruit—such as a dried cherry—inside the coconut dough before baking.

3 tablespoons flaxseed meal

¼ cup + 2 tablespoons water

4 cups sweetened shredded coconut

¼ cup cocoa powder

½ cup sugar

½ teaspoon salt

- Preheat oven to 350°F and line a cookie sheet with a silicone mat or parchment paper.

- In a small bowl, whisk together the flaxseed meal and water and let set for 5 minutes, until gelled. In a medium bowl, stir together the remaining ingredients until blended. Fold in the prepared flaxseed meal and stir well until completely incorporated. The batter will be slightly tricky to squeeze together but will hold well once baked. Drop by tablespoons onto the prepared cookie sheet and bake for 15 to 18 minutes, until fragrant and slightly darkened.

- Let rest for at least 1 hour before serving.

# FLORENTINES

**YIELD: 12 COOKIES**

Even though the name sounds wholly Italian, these cookies most likely originated in French kitchens, with the name simply a nod to the Tuscan city. As beautiful as they are tasty, don't be intimidated by the Florentine; they are a snap to make. Be sure to leave extra space in between each cookie, as they spread! Aim for about six per standard-size cookie sheet.

1¼ cups sliced almonds

¼ cup superfine brown rice flour

⅓ cup sugar

4 tablespoons non dairy margarine

¼ cup agave

¼ teaspoon salt

56

⅓ cup non dairy chocolate, melted

2 tablespoons finely chopped <u>Candied Orange Peels</u> or orange zest

- Preheat oven to 350°F.

- In a medium bowl, combine the almonds and the brown rice flour. In a small saucepan, mix together the sugar, margarine, agave, and salt and bring to a boil, stirring often. Remove immediately from heat and stir mixture into the almond mixture. Mix until totally combined and drop by heaping tablespoons onto a parchment-lined cookie sheet, about 3 inches apart. Using a lightly greased fork, press down cookies into a flat circle, so that the almonds are in a single layer.

- Bake for 5 minutes, rotate the cookie sheet, and bake for 4 to 5 minutes more, until the edges of the cookies are golden brown. Let cool completely and then drizzle with melted chocolate and sprinkle with orange peel. Let chocolate firm up before serving. Store in airtight container for up to 1 week.

# THUMBPRINT COOKIES

**YIELD: 24 COOKIES**

A lovely cookie that is simple to make and easy on the eyes. Sprinkle with confectioners sugar once cooled for an elegant presentation. This cookie works best with low-sugar preserves (my favorites are apricot and raspberry!) or a high-pectin jam. Other types of jams can cause the filling to spread.

1 tablespoon flaxseed meal

2 tablespoons water

1 cup non dairy margarine

1 cup sugar

1 teaspoon vanilla extract

1 teaspoon baking powder

1 cup sorghum flour

1 cup potato starch

1 cup almond meal

1 teaspoon xanthan gum

⅓ cup preserves (1 teaspoon per cookie)

- Preheat oven to 350°F.
- Mix the flaxseed meal with the water in a very small bowl. Let rest for 5 minutes, or until gelled. Line a cookie sheet with parchment

paper or a silicone baking mat.

- Cream together the margarine and sugar until smooth. Add in the prepared flaxseed meal and vanilla extract and mix well.

- In a separate bowl, combine the baking powder, sorghum flour, potato starch, almond meal, and xanthan gum.

- Gradually add the flour mixture into the sugar mixture until a stiff dough forms.

- Shape into 1-inch balls and place onto cookie sheet. Use the back of a ½ teaspoon (or your thumb) to make an indent in the cookies while slightly flattening them.

- Fill each cookie with a little less than a teaspoon of preserves. Bake for 15 minutes in preheated oven and then let cool completely. Store in airtight container for up to 4 days.

# MEXICAN WEDDING COOKIES

**YIELD: 15 COOKIES**

These delicately crunchy cookies practically melt in your mouth. Also known as Russian Tea Cakes or Polvorones, it doesn't matter what name you use— once you try them, you'll never forget them.

¾ cup non dairy margarine

½ cup confectioner's sugar, plus ¼ cup for rolling

½ teaspoon salt

1 cup almond meal

1½ teaspoons vanilla extract

¾ cup sorghum flour

½ cup potato starch

¼ cup tapioca flour

1 teaspoon xanthan gum

- Preheat oven to 325°F.

- In a large mixing bowl, cream together the margarine and ½ cup confectioner's sugar until smooth. Add the salt, almond meal, and vanilla extract and mix well. In a separate bowl, whisk together the sorghum flour, potato starch, tapioca flour, and xanthan gum.

- Gradually incorporate the flour mixture into the margarine mixture until a clumpy dough forms. Shape into 1-inch balls and place onto an ungreased cookie sheet.

- Bake for 17 to 20 minutes in a preheated oven. Let cool for 2 to 3 minutes, then coat the entire cookie with the additional confectioner's sugar. Let cool completely before serving. Store in airtight container for up to 2 weeks.

# CRANBERRY WHITE CHOCOLATE ORANGE CLUSTERS

**YIELD: 24 COOKIES**

These soft clusters of fragrant citrus, tangy cranberry, and creamy white chocolate will have you reaching in the cookie jar again and again!

2 tablespoons flaxseed meal

4 tablespoons water

½ cup non dairy margarine

½ cup unsweetened applesauce

1 cup sugar

1 teaspoon vanilla extract

½ teaspoon orange zest

1 teaspoon salt

1 teaspoon baking soda

1½ cups superfine or regular brown rice flour

1 cup cornstarch

½ cup tapioca flour

1 teaspoon xanthan gum

½ cup dried cranberries

½ cup non dairy white chocolate chips

- Preheat oven to 375°F.

- In a small bowl, mix together the flaxseed meal and the water and let rest until gelled, for about 5 minutes.

- In a large mixing bowl, cream together the margarine, applesauce, sugar, vanilla extract, and orange zest until smooth. In a medium bowl, whisk together the salt, baking soda, brown rice flour, cornstarch, tapioca flour, and xanthan gum. Gradually incorporate into the sugar mixture until a soft dough forms. Fold in the cranberries and white chocolate chips.

- Drop by the tablespoonful onto a parchment-lined cookie sheet, about 2 inches apart. Bake for 12 to 15 minutes, until golden brown on edges. Let cool completely before serving. Store in airtight container for up to 1 week.

# DATE DROP COOKIES

**YIELD: 24 COOKIES**

Sticky sweet centers are enveloped in a soft cookie to bring you an ultimate treat. My husband, who is admittedly a cookie fanatic, raves about these guys and their irresistible texture. I particularly like them because they are simple to prepare but look so beautiful when baked. For soy-free cookies, use soy- free yogurt.

## FILLING

1¼ cup dates, pitted and finely chopped

½ cup water Pinch salt

## COOKIES

2 tablespoons ground flaxseed

4 tablespoons water

1 cup non dairy margarine

¾ cup sugar

¾ cup brown sugar

⅓ cup plain unsweetened non dairy yogurt

1 teaspoon vanilla extract

1¼ cups sorghum flour

1 cup superfine brown rice flour

¾ cup cornstarch

¼ cup sweet white rice flour

1 teaspoon xanthan gum

1¼ teaspoons baking soda

½ teaspoon salt


- Place filling ingredients into a 2-quart saucepan and heat over medium heat, stirring often. Cook mixture for 5 minutes, or until thickened. Set aside.

- Preheat oven to 400°F.

- In a small bowl, combine the flaxseed meal with water and allow to gel for 5 minutes, or until thick. In a large mixing bowl, cream together the margarine and sugars until smooth. Add in the prepared flaxseed meal, yogurt, and vanilla extract. In a separate bowl, whisk together the rest of the ingredients. Gradually incorporate the flour mixture into the sugar mixture until a clumpy dough forms.

- On an ungreased cookie sheet, drop a tablespoon of the dough. Next, place a teaspoon of the date filling on top of the dough, and then top with a teaspoon more cookie dough. Repeat with all dough and filling. Bake for 11 minutes; let cool completely before serving. Store in airtight container for up to 1 week.

# PEANUT BUTTER CHOCOLATE NO-BAKE COOKIES

**YIELD: 24 COOKIES**

This is one of the very first recipes I learned to make as a kid, and boy did I make them a lot! These were always a favorite due to their quickness and ease and irresistible chocolate peanut butter combo.

¼ cup cocoa powder

2 cups sugar

½ cup almond milk

½ cup non dairy margarine

½ cup + 3 tablespoons creamy peanut butter

1 teaspoon vanilla extract

3½ cups certified gluten-free oats

- Line a large cookie tray with parchment paper.

- In a 2-quart saucepan, combine the cocoa powder, sugar, almond milk, and margarine. Bring to a boil over medium heat, stirring often. Boil for exactly

67

2 minutes and then remove from heat. Immediately stir in the peanut butter and vanilla extract. Fold in the oats and then drop by spoonfuls on prepared cookie tray. Let rest until firm, for about 1 to 2 hours. Store in airtight container for up to 1 week.

# CHERRY COCONUT NO-BAKE COOKIES

**YIELD: 24 COOKIES**

Tart cherries work so nicely with the base of these no-bakes—perfect for when you're craving cookies, but don't want to turn on the oven.

2 cups sugar

¼ cup coconut oil

2 teaspoons vanilla extract

½ cup non dairy milk

3 cups certified gluten-free oats

⅓ cup dried cherries

½ cup unsweetened flaked coconut

¼ cup almond meal

- Line a large cookie tray with parchment paper.

- In a 2-quart saucepan, over medium heat, combine the sugar, coconut oil, vanilla extract, and nondairy milk. While stirring often, bring the mixture to a boil. Once boiling, continue cooking over medium heat, stirring occasionally, for 1½ to 2 minutes. Remove the mixture from heat and stir in

69

oats, cherries, coconut, and almond meal.

- Drop by heaping tablespoonfuls onto the prepared cookie sheet. While the cookies are still warm, guide them into an evenly round shape using lightly greased fingertips.

- Let the cookies cool for about 1 hour at room temperature. They will harden up nicely.

- Store in airtight container for up to 2 weeks.

# BLACK AND WHITE COOKIES

**YIELD: 12 COOKIES**

If you've never tried a black and white cookie, you are in for a treat. These ginormous lemony beasts boast not one, but two flavors of icing: chocolate *and* vanilla.

½ cup + 1 tablespoon non dairy margarine

¾ cup sugar

½ teaspoon lemon oil or extract

2 teaspoons egg replacer powder (such as Orgran) mixed with 2 tablespoons water

1 cup besan/chickpea flour

½ cup white rice flour

½ cup potato starch

1 teaspoon xanthan gum

½ teaspoon baking powder

¼ teaspoon salt

⅔ cup non dairy milk

1 recipe Chocolate Glaze

1 recipe Vanilla Glaze

- Preheat oven to 350°F. Line a large baking sheet with parchment paper.

- Cream together the margarine and sugar in a large mixing bowl. Add in the lemon oil and prepared egg replacer. In a separate bowl, whisk together the besan, white rice flour, potato starch, xanthan gum, baking powder, and salt. Add it to the margarine mixture and then add in the nondairy milk. Stir well to combine until a fluffy cookie dough is formed. Using an ice cream scoop, drop dough in 3-ounce balls onto the prepared cookie sheet, leaving about 4 inches between each cookie. You will have to make these in multiple batches as they need room to spread.

- Bake for 22 minutes, or until edges are light golden brown. Remove from the oven and let cool completely. Prepare the Vanilla Glaze and frost one half of each of the cookies with the vanilla glaze. Let harden for about 20 minutes, and prepare the Chocolate Glaze. Frost the other half of each cookie with the chocolate glaze. Let harden completely, for about 2 hours, before serving. Store in airtight container for up to 3 days.

# GINGER SNAPPERS

**YIELD: 24 COOKIES**

Crispier than gingerbread, these snappers pack a big ginger flavor into such a small little snack.

1 tablespoon flaxseed meal

2 tablespoons water

1 cup packed light brown sugar

¾ cup olive oil

¼ cup molasses

1 cup sorghum flour

¼ cup superfine brown rice flour

½ cup potato starch

¼ cup tapioca flour

1 teaspoon xanthan gum

2 teaspoons baking soda

1 teaspoon salt

1 teaspoon cinnamon

2 teaspoons fresh grated ginger

½ teaspoon cloves

⅓ cup turbinado sugar, for rolling

- In a small bowl, combine the flaxseed meal with water and let rest until gelled, for about 5 minutes. Preheat oven to 375°F.

- In a large bowl, mix together the brown sugar, olive oil, molasses, and prepared flaxseed meal.

- In a smaller bowl, whisk together the rest of the ingredients except for the turbinado sugar, and, once mixed, gradually incorporate into the sugar mixture until a stiff dough forms.

- Roll into 1-inch balls and then coat with turbinado sugar. Flatten slightly using the bottom of a glass and bake for 13 minutes in preheated oven. Let cool completely before serving. Store in airtight container for up to 2 weeks.

# LEMON OLIVE OIL COOKIES

**YIELD: 24 COOKIES**

Tender and bright, these cookies are sure to delight! Use freshly squeezed lemon juice and extra-virgin olive oil for best results. If the dough seems a little soft, be sure to chill for about 20 minutes in the refrigerator before baking to prevent excessive spreading.

1 cup sorghum flour

¾ cup brown rice flour

½ cup potato starch

¼ cup almond meal

1 teaspoon xanthan gum

1¼ cups sugar

2 teaspoons baking soda

½ teaspoon salt

2 teaspoons lemon zest

½ cup olive oil

½ cup lemon juice

Granulated sugar for garnishing

- Preheat oven to 350°F.

- In a large bowl, whisk the sorghum flour, brown rice flour, potato starch, almond meal, xanthan gum, sugar, baking soda, and salt. Mix in the lemon zest, olive oil, and lemon juice until a thick cookie dough forms.

- Drop the dough by heaping tablespoonfuls, or roll dough into walnut-size balls and place about 2 inches apart onto an ungreased baking sheet.

- Flatten slightly with a fork (like you would with a peanut butter cookie) and sprinkle lightly with granulated sugar.

- Bake in your preheated oven for 12 minutes, or until edges are slightly golden brown.

- Remove from oven and let cool completely before serving. Store in airtight container for up to 1 week.

# ROLLED AND SHAPED COOKIES

# VANILLA WAFERS

**YIELD: ABOUT 36 COOKIES**

A vanilla wafer is always a good cookie to have around for basic reasons, like making into cookie crumbs, using in trifles, and simply snacking. Use the highest-quality vanilla extract you can get your hands on for these, or better yet, make your own.

1 tablespoon flaxseed meal

2 tablespoons water

5 tablespoons non dairy margarine

1 cup sugar

1 tablespoon vanilla extract

¼ cup non dairy milk

¾ cup sorghum flour

½ cup white rice flour

½ cup potato starch

¼ cup tapioca flour

1 teaspoon xanthan gum

2 teaspoons baking powder

¼ teaspoon salt

- Preheat oven to 350°F and line a cookie sheet with parchment paper.

- In a small bowl, stir together the flaxseed meal and water and let rest until gelled, for about 5 minutes.

- In a separate bowl, cream together the margarine, sugar, and vanilla extract until smooth. Mix in the prepared flaxseed meal and nondairy milk.

- In a medium bowl, whisk together the remaining ingredients and then combine well with the margarine mixture until a soft dough forms. Place into a large freezer bag and snip off the tip. Pipe out 1-inch circles onto the parchment-covered cookie sheet about 1 inch apart. Bake for about 20 minutes, or until golden brown on edges. Let cool completely before serving. Store in airtight container for up to 2 weeks.

# CHOCOLATE WAFERS

**YIELD: 36 COOKIES**

Just as versatile as their vanilla cousins, these wafers can wear many hats. Sandwich a little Caramel Frosting in between two cookies or add 1 teaspoon mint extract and dip them in melted chocolate for easy thin mints.

¾ cup cold non dairy margarine

1 cup sugar

1 cup sorghum flour

¾ cup cocoa powder

½ cup potato starch

1 teaspoon xanthan gum

¼ teaspoon baking soda

2 tablespoons strong coffee

¼ cup additional cocoa powder

- Preheat oven to 350°F. Line a large cookie sheet with parchment paper or a silicone baking mat.

- In a large bowl, cream together the margarine and sugar until smooth. In a separate bowl, whisk together the sorghum flour, cocoa powder, potato starch, xanthan gum, and baking soda. Fold the dry ingredients into the sugar mixture and mix until crumbly. Add the coffee and mix until a soft dough

81

forms.

- Gradually fold in the ¼ cup cocoa powder and mix just until dough is workable. Chill in freezer for 5 to 10 minutes and then pinch off sections large enough to create 1-inch balls. Place dough balls onto the prepared baking sheet and flatten with the bottom of a glass to about ¼ inch thick. Bake for 16 minutes. Allow to cool completely before serving. Store in airtight container to keep crisp for up to 2 weeks.

# SUGAR COOKIES

**YIELD: 24 COOKIE**

Sometimes a basic sugar cookie is the best dessert! The secret to these cookies is to keep the dough chilled. I like them best rolled to ¼ inch thick, but you can roll them a touch thinner if you prefer a crispier sugar cookie.

¾ cup non dairy margarine

½ cup sugar

½ cup confectioners sugar

3 teaspoons powdered egg replacer + 2 tablespoons hot water, frothed with fork

2 tablespoons apple cider vinegar

1 teaspoon vanilla extract 1 cup sorghum flour

½ cup white rice flour

¾ cup potato starch

½ cup tapioca flour

1 teaspoon xanthan gum

1 teaspoon baking powder

- Cream together the margarine and sugars until smooth. Mix in the prepared egg replacer along with the vinegar and vanilla extract.

- In a separate bowl, whisk together the sorghum flour, white rice flour, potato starch, tapioca flour, xanthan gum, and baking powder. Gradually combine the flour mixture with the margarine mixture until a clumpy dough forms. If the dough seems too sticky to handle, add a little more sorghum flour … it should be easily workable with your hands, yet a little bit sticky. Form into a patty, wrap in plastic wrap, and chill until cold, for about 1 hour in the refrigerator and 15 minutes in the freezer.

- When your dough is chilled, preheat oven to 400°F. Lay countertop or other work area with parchment paper, and using a lightly floured (any kind of flour will do) rolling pin, roll dough anywhere between ⅓ to ½ inch thick. Cut out using your favorite cookie cutters, and use a flat metal spatula to gently lift the cookies and place them onto an ungreased cookie sheet. Repeat until all dough is used. If the dough seems to be getting a little soft and sticks to your pin, rechill until once again workable.

- Bake cookies for 7 to 8 minutes, or until slightly golden brown on edges. Remove from oven and let cool completely before handling. Store in airtight container for up to 1 week.

- Once they have fully cooled, eat as is or cover them with icing! Royal Icing works beautifully here. Pipe a ring around the cookie's exterior and let harden before filling it in with icing. This will ensure an even layer of icing on the tops with no drips.

# BUTTERY SHORTBREAD

**YIELD: ABOUT 20 COOKIES**

Shortbread used to be considered a delicacy and was reserved for special occasions, such as Christmas or weddings. But no need to wait for a holiday, whip some of these cookies up anytime a craving strikes. This simple cookie can be made extra fancy if you bake them in shortbread molds and dip the ends in melted chocolate.

1 tablespoon flaxseed meal

2 tablespoons water

½ cup + 2 tablespoons non dairy margarine

½ cup sugar

1 teaspoon vanilla extract

¾ cup sorghum flour

¼ cup brown rice flour

¼ cup tapioca flour

½ cup arrowroot starch

¼ cup sweet white rice flour

1 teaspoon xanthan gum

½ cup non dairy chocolate chips, melted, for dipping (optional)

* In a small bowl, combine the flaxseed meal with water and let rest until gelled, for about 5 minutes. In a large mixing bowl, cream together the margarine

and the sugar until smooth. Add in the prepared flaxseed meal and vanilla extract and mix until combined.

- In a separate bowl, whisk together the sorghum flour, brown rice flour, tapioca flour, arrowroot starch, sweet white rice flour, and xanthan gum. Gradually mix into the sugar mixture until a clumpy dough forms. The dough may be crumbly at first, but allow enough mixing time for it to come together.

- Wrap the dough in parchment paper and chill for about 30 minutes in the freezer. The dough should be cold, but workable; if it is too crumbly once removed from the freezer, work it a bit with your hands to soften it up.

- Preheat oven to 350°F.

- Create a disk with the dough and place in between two sheets of plastic wrap and roll out to a ¼ inch thickness. Cut using a bench scraper into 2-inch squares, or use a circle cookie cutter, and place onto an ungreased cookie sheet. Bake for 12 minutes, or until bottoms are slightly golden brown. Let cool completely before removing from cookie sheet. At this point, if desired, the cookies can be dipped in melted chocolate and allowed to set backup on a sheet of waxed paper. Store in airtight container for up to 2 weeks.

# CHOCOLATE SHORTBREAD

**YIELD: 12 COOKIES**

Just like the traditional shortbread, only much more chocolaty. I like to cut these into bars, but feel free to shape them as you desire with metal cookie cutters.

1 cup non dairy margarine

½ cup + 2 tablespoons sugar, plus ¼ cup for rolling

½ cup cocoa powder

¾ cup sorghum flour

¾ cup brown rice flour

½ cup potato starch

1 teaspoon xanthan gum

- Cream together the margarine and ½ cup + 2 tablespoons sugar until smooth. Using an electric mixer, or mixing quickly with a spoon, gradually add the cocoa powder.

- In a separate bowl, combine the sorghum flour, brown rice flour, potato starch, and xanthan gum. Add the flour mixture into the sugar mixture (a little bit at a time) until all is incorporated.

- Keep mixing until a stiff dough forms, scraping down the sides as necessary. It will look crumbly at first, but will come together nicely with a little mixing. Using your hands, pat dough into a disk on a lightly sugared surface and then chill the dough in the refrigerator for 2 to 3 hours.

- When you're ready to bake the cookies, preheat oven to 300°F.

- Use a large knife to cut the dough into even rectangles, about 1 × 4 inches. Using a flat  metal spatula, scoop up cookies and place them onto an ungreased cookie sheet. Sprinkle with granulated sugar and then poke a few holes in the tops with a fork. Bake for 30 to 35 minutes. Let cool completely before serving. Store in airtight container for up to 2 weeks.

# SPECULOOS

**YIELD: 24 COOKIES**

These cookies have been a favorite of mine long before I ever knew what a speculoos was. I learned this term from the vegan blogging world but soon realized it had been one of my favorites since childhood, only I knew these spicy treats as "windmill cookies." Feel free to roll these out flat and cut with windmill cutters to share in my nostalgia.

1 tablespoon flaxseed meal

2 tablespoons water

1 cup sorghum flour

¼ cup tapioca flour

¼ cup potato starch

½ cup + 2 tablespoons almond meal

1 teaspoon xanthan gum

1 teaspoon baking powder

1 teaspoon cinnamon

¼ teaspoon cloves

¼ teaspoon nutmeg

¼ teaspoon fresh ground ginger

¼ teaspoon salt

½ cup non dairy margarine

¾ cup packed light brown sugar

Extra sugar for sprinkling (optional)

Sliced almonds for topping

- In a small bowl, combine the flaxseed meal with water and let rest until gelled, for about 5 minutes.

- In a large bowl, whisk together all the flour ingredients (up until the margarine) until well blended. In a separate mixing bowl, cream together the margarine and brown sugar until smooth. Mix in the prepared flaxseed meal until a smooth mixture is formed. Gradually add in the flour mixture and mix for about 45 seconds at medium speed until the dough clumps together. Chill in the freezer for 40 minutes, or until stiff—or alternatively, chill in refrigerator overnight.

- Preheat oven to 350°F. Once the dough is chilled, use your hands to roll into 1-inch wide balls and place onto an ungreased cookie sheet. Flatten with the bottom of a glass— slightly damp and dipped in granulated sugar. Top with a few sliced almonds and bake in preheated oven for 15 minutes. Let cool on the cookie sheet before attempting to move. Once cool, transfer to wire rack to fully harden.

- Store in airtight container for up to 5 days.

# SPECULOOS BUTTER

**YIELD: ABOUT 2 CUPS**

This cookie butter has taken over the nation from suppliers such as Trader Joe's popularizing it to the extreme … but I've never found one in stores that is gluten-free! So, I had to make my own, and boy am I glad I did. Try this "butter" on top of cupcakes, more cookies, ice cream, or simply a spoon.

24 Speculoos cookies

3 tablespoons water

½ cup coconut oil, melted

- Place the cookies into a food processor and pulse until very crumbly. Make sure the crumbles are finely chopped. Add in the water, one tablespoon at a time and pulse until well blended. Drizzle in the coconut oil and let blend until very smooth, for about 5 minutes, scraping the sides as needed. Transfer into a jar and store in refrigerator. Keep for up to 2 weeks.

# PIZZELLES

**YIELD: 18 COOKIE**

These cookies are delicious on their own but also make a fabulous accompaniment to ice cream, especially when shaped into waffle cones. To make these cookies into homemade waffle cones you will need a Pizzelle press, which can be sourced from any typical home goods store. When hot to the touch, shape the cookie disks into cones, fit inside a small bowl to make waffle bowls; or, leave them flat for classic pizzelle cookies.

3 tablespoons flaxseed meal

6 tablespoons water

1 cup white rice flour

½ cup potato starch

¼ cup tapioca flour

2 teaspoons baking powder

1 teaspoon xanthan gum

1 teaspoon vanilla extract

1 cup melted non dairy margarine

¼ cup water

- Preheat the pizzelle press and grease lightly with oil or nonstick spray just before the first batch, and repeat sparingly as needed.

- In a small bowl, mix the flaxseed meal with water and let rest for 5 minutes, until gelled. In a medium bowl, whisk together the rice flour, potato starch, tapioca flour, baking powder, and xanthan gum. Make a well in the center of the flours and add in the vanilla extract, melted margarine, prepared flaxseed meal, and water. Mix until smooth. Place about 1 tablespoon batter onto the hot press and clamp down to close. Cook until golden brown and then gently remove.

- To make waffle cones: Using an oven mitt or heat-safe gloved hands, gently shape the cookie into a cone and snugly place in a safe spot to cool, for about 1 hour. Watch that they don't unravel before cooling or they will become stuck in that shape. Let cool completely, and then serve with your favorite frozen treat. Store in airtight container for up to 3 weeks.

# SNOW CAP COOKIES

**YIELD: 24 COOKIES**

These cookies are a classic right up there next to Chocolate Chip and Peanut Butter. This version includes teff flour, which boasts a pretty impressive nutritional profile for such a tiny grain, being high in protein, iron, calcium, and potassium!

3 tablespoons flaxseed meal

6 tablespoons water

1 cup cocoa powder

½ cup teff flour

¾ cup sorghum flour

¼ cup tapioca flour

½ cup potato starch

1 teaspoon xanthan gum

2 teaspoons baking powder

½ teaspoon salt 2 cups sugar

½ cup melted non hydrogenated shortening

¼ cup non dairy milk

½ cup confectioners sugar

* In a small bowl, combine the flaxseed meal with water and let rest until gelled,

for about 5 minutes.

- In a large bowl, whisk together the cocoa powder, teff flour, sorghum flour, tapioca flour, potato starch, xanthan gum, baking powder, salt, and sugar. While stirring constantly, or set on medium speed of an electric mixer, add in the prepared flaxseed meal and shortening until a crumbly dough forms. Mix well to blend. Add in the nondairy milk while continuing to stir and keep mixing until the dough clumps together easily.

- Wrap dough in parchment or foil and chill in refrigerator for 2 hours.

- Once chilled, roll into small balls about 1½ inches wide and flatten slightly to resemble small pucks.

- Preheat oven to 350°F.

- Dip the tops only in confectioner's sugar and place onto an ungreased cookie sheet. Bake for 12 minutes, or until spread out and crackled. The centers will still be gooey while warm. Allow to cool completely before enjoying. Store in airtight container for up to 1 week.

# TUXEDO SANDWICH COOKIES

These cookies taste just like America's favorite sandwich cookie; a touch of orange adds an elegant note. You can even twist off the tops and just enjoy the filling! Dunked in almond milk they become the perfect remedy to the midday slumps.

## COOKIES

1 cup non dairy margarine

¾ cup sugar

¼ cup brown sugar

1 teaspoon vanilla extract

¾ cup dark cocoa powder

½ cup superfine brown rice flour

1 cup sorghum flour

½ cup potato starch

1½ teaspoons xanthan gum

1 teaspoon salt

1 teaspoon baking powder

½ teaspoon baking soda

## FILLING

1½ tablespoons orange zest

½ cup very cold coconut-based buttery spread (shortening will also work)

½ cup non dairy margarine

3½ cups confectioner's sugar

- Cream together the margarine and sugars and then mix in the vanilla extract. In a separate bowl, whisk together the cocoa powder, superfine brown rice flour, sorghum flour, potato starch, xanthan gum, salt, baking powder, and baking soda.

- Gradually incorporate the flours with the margarine mixture until a clumpy dark dough is formed. Divide and pat into two disks. Chill in the refrigerator for 2 hours, or briefly in freezer, for about 10 minutes.

- After dough is chilled, preheat oven to 350°F and line two cookie sheets with parchment paper. On a flat surface, place each chilled disk of dough between two separate sheets of parchment paper and roll each disk to about ⅛ inch thickness. Using a round 2-inch cookie cutter, cut out circles of dough and transfer onto prepared cookie sheets. Bake for 13 minutes and let cool completely before piping filling in between two of the cookies.

- To make the filling, simply mix together all frosting ingredients using an electric mixer with whisk attachment. Whip until fluffy and then pipe a ring onto one cookie and smoosh down with another until an even layer of frosting is snugly set in the middle. Store in airtight container for up to 1 week.

# COCONUT CARAMEL COOKIES

**YIELD: 24 COOKIES**

Similar to the coconut-topped Girl Scout Cookies that are both chewy and crisp, these brilliant bites utilize Medjool dates to stand in for the caramel, adding a little extra goodness.

## COOKIES

1 cup non dairy margarine

1 teaspoon vanilla extract

½ cup sugar

1 cup sorghum flour

¾ cup superfine brown rice flour

¾ cup potato starch

1½ teaspoons xanthan gum

## TOPPING

20 Medjool dates, pits removed

4 tablespoons non dairy margarine

1 teaspoon vanilla extract

½ teaspoon sea salt

3 tablespoons water

2 cups toasted coconut shreds

2 cups chopped non dairy chocolate

- Cream together the margarine, vanilla extract, and sugar until smooth. In a separate bowl, mix together sorghum flour, brown rice flour, potato starch, and xanthan gum.

- Using an electric mixer, slowly incorporate flour mixture into the margarine mixture and beat on medium-low speed for about 2 minutes, scraping sides as needed to form a stiff dough. Press dough into a disk and chill in refrigerator for an hour or so, or chill in the freezer for about 30 minutes.

- Preheat oven to 300°F.

- Once dough has chilled, roll out gently onto parchment paper. The warmer the dough becomes the softer it will get. Roll to about ½ inch thick. Using a 1½-inch circular cookie cutter, cut out as many circles as possible, saving the scraps, rechilling and rerolling until no dough remains. Cut the centers of the cookies out using a small circular cookie cutter, or the back of an icing tip.

- Place cookies gently onto a parchment-covered cookie sheet and bake for 30 to 35 minutes, or until very lightly golden on edges. Let cool completely before removing from cookie sheet.

- Put dates, margarine, vanilla extract, sea salt, and water into a food processor and blend until very smooth, scraping down sides often. Stir in the toasted coconut. Transfer the mixture into a piping bag fitted with a very wide tip. Pipe a ring of filling carefully onto the cookies and press gently into place using slightly greased fingers. Place upside down onto a piece of waxed paper or silicone mat.

- In a double boiler, place the chocolate into the bowl and warm over medium-low heat until melted. Brush the tops of the inverted cookies with melted chocolate to completely coat. Let the chocolate harden and then flip the cookies over. Drizzle with stripes of chocolate and let harden again. Store in airtight container for up to 1 week.

# LEMON SANDWICH COOKIES

**YIELD: 24 COOKIES**

These dreamy cookies, with crispy wafers and creamy filling, make a wonderful accompaniment to chamomile or green tea.

COOKIES

1 tablespoon flaxseed meal

2 tablespoons water

1⅓ cups superfine brown rice flour

½ cup sorghum flour

¼ cup tapioca flour

½ cup potato starch

1½ teaspoons xanthan gum

¾ teaspoon baking powder

½ teaspoon salt

1 cup sugar

½ cup non dairy margarine

¼ cup lemon juice

Zest of 1 lemon

FILLING

1 teaspoon lemon zest

1 tablespoon lemon juice

½ cup shortening

½ cup non dairy margarine

3½ cups + 2 tablespoons confectioners sugar

- In a small bowl, combine the flaxseed meal with water and let rest until gelled, for about 5 minutes.

- In a medium bowl, whisk together the superfine brown rice flour, sorghum flour, tapioca flour, potato starch, xanthan gum, baking powder, and salt.

- In a large bowl, cream together the sugar and the margarine until smooth. Add the prepared flaxseed meal, lemon juice, and lemon zest and mix well. Slowly incorporate the flour mixture and stir well until a stiff dough forms. Divide dough into two equal-size disks and chill for at least 1 hour in refrigerator. When dough is chilled, preheat oven to 375°F. Roll out one section of dough in between two sheets of parchment paper until about ¼ inch thick. Using a circular cookie cutter, cut out cookies and place onto an ungreased cookie sheet. Repeat until all dough has been used, rechilling the dough if it becomes too soft to work with.

- Bake in preheated oven for 9 minutes. Let cool completely. Make the filling by mixing together all the ingredients in a mixer at high speed until very well combined. Pipe filling onto the back of one cookie and sandwich together with another cookie. Repeat until all cookies have been filled.

- Allow cookies to set for at least 1 hour for best flavor and texture. Store in airtight container for up to 1 week.

# ROLLED GINGERBREAD COOKIES

**YIELD: 24 COOKIES**

Freshly grated ginger really makes these cookies sparkle. Feel free to cut these little guys (or gals) into any shape your heart desires. Roll them thicker for softer cookies, and thinner for crispier.

1 tablespoon flaxseed meal

2 tablespoons water

½ cup non dairy margarine

½ cup sugar

½ cup molasses

1 teaspoon freshly grated ginger

1 teaspoon cinnamon

½ teaspoon nutmeg

½ teaspoon cloves

1¾ cups buckwheat flour, divided

¾ cup potato starch

¼ cup tapioca flour

1 teaspoon xanthan gum

½ teaspoon salt

- In a small bowl, stir together the flaxseed meal and water and allow to rest for 5 minutes, until gelled.

- In a large mixing bowl, cream together the margarine, sugar, molasses, ginger, and prepared flaxseed meal. In a separate bowl, whisk together the spices, 1 cup buckwheat flour, potato starch, tapioca flour, xanthan gum, and salt. Add into the sugar mixture and mix until a dough forms. Add up to ¾ cup additional buckwheat flour, until a soft dough that is easy to handle forms. Gently pat the dough into a disk and wrap in parchment paper. Place in freezer and chill for 30 minutes.

- When the dough is chilled, preheat oven to 350°F. Divide dough in half, and roll out one half of dough (while chilling the other half) to about ¼ inch thick. Work fast so the dough stays chilled; the warmer the dough gets, the stickier it becomes. Once rolled, use your favorite cookie cutters to cut out shapes and place the cut cookies directly onto a parchment-covered baking sheet. Bake for 9 minutes. Repeat with the remaining dough and then let cool.

- Decorate with Royal Icing. Store in airtight container for up to 2 weeks.

# FIGGY FILLED COOKIES

**YIELD: 24 COOKIES**

These delightful cookies, similar to commercial fig bars, are hearty and not-too-sweet. The key to these cookies is keeping the dough super cold. I advise chilling after each rolling and shaping to ensure stick-free, evenly rolled cookies with no frustration.

## COOKIE DOUGH

1½ tablespoons flaxseed meal

3 tablespoons water

⅔ cup cold non dairy margarine

1 cup sugar

1 teaspoon vanilla extract

1⅔ cups brown rice flour

⅔ cup potato starch

⅓ cup tapioca flour

1 teaspoon xanthan gum

2½ teaspoons baking powder

⅓ cup non dairy milk

Additional brown rice flour for rolling

# FILLING

2¼ cups dried mission figs, tops removed

¼ cup raisins

1 teaspoon orange zest

1 small apple, diced

½ cup pecans

3 tablespoons sugar

1 teaspoon cinnamon

- In a small bowl, combine the flaxseed meal with the water and let rest for about 5 minutes, until gelled.

- In a large mixing bowl, cream together the margarine and sugar until smooth. Mix in the vanilla extract and prepared flaxseed meal.

- In a separate, smaller, bowl, whisk together the brown rice flour, potato starch, tapioca flour, xanthan gum, and baking powder. Gradually add the flour mixture to the sugar mixture and stir well to combine. Add the nondairy milk and mix until a soft dough forms. Dust lightly with brown rice flour if sticky. Wrap in parchment paper and chill in freezer for about 15 minutes, until cold.

- Place all ingredients for the filling into a food processor and pulse until finely crumbled and sticky, scraping down the sides of the bowl as needed.

- Preheat oven to 375°F.

- Take about one-third of the chilled dough and roll it out (in between two sheets of parchment paper) into a rectangle about 3½ inches wide and about ¼ inch thick. Chill briefly, for about 5 minutes in freezer. Roll out a long snake of filling, as you would clay, about 1 inch wide, and place into the center of the rectangle. Fold over each side of the dough, like wrapping a present, using parchment to help roll it up and over, and seal gently using your fingertips. You should have a slightly flat, long enclosed dough tube of figgy filling.

- Chill again briefly, for about 5 minutes. Flip filled dough over to hide the seam on the bottom.

- Using a very clean, sharp, flat blade, cut into 2-inch sections, so that you end up with shapes that look like a popular store-bought variety of fig cookies. Place 2 inches apart onto a parchment-lined cookie sheet. Bake for 15 to 17 minutes or until slightly golden brown on edges. Store in airtight container for up to 1 week.

# SPRINGERLES

**YIELD: 30 COOKIES**

These cookies taste wonderful with or without the use of a Springerle mold, so feel free to let them remain flat on top if you don't have molds handy.

¾ cup non dairy margarine

1 cup sugar

1 teaspoon anise extract

2½ teaspoons powdered egg replacer, such as Orgran or EnerG, mixed with 3 tablespoons water

1 cup superfine brown rice flour

½ cup millet flour

1 cup potato starch

¼ cup tapioca flour

1 teaspoon xanthan gum

1 teaspoon baking powder

½ teaspoon baking soda

¼ teaspoon salt

- Preheat oven to 350°F. In a large bowl, cream together the margarine, sugar, and anise extract. Add the prepared egg replacer.

- In a separate bowl, whisk together the rest of the ingredients. Gradually add into the margarine mixture and mix very well until a clumpy dough forms. Roll dough out to about ½ inch thickness. Lightly dust a Springerle mold with superfine brown rice flour, emboss a pattern into the tops of the dough, and then cut cookies to size with a knife. Carefully transfer onto an ungreased baking sheet. Let rest for 1 hour, and then bake for 15 minutes, until very lightly browned on edges and bottoms. To prevent cracking, prop your oven door open an inch or so while baking. Let cool completely before using a spatula to remove. Store in airtight container for up to 1 week.

# CINNAMON GRAHAM CRACKERS

**YIELD: 30 CRACKERS**

A perfect base for so many recipes, such as s'mores or cheesecake crusts, these crispy crackers are also pretty great on their own. These are especially good slathered with a bit of almond or coconut butter.

1 cup buckwheat flour

1 cup superfine brown rice flour

¼ cup tapioca flour

¾ cup cornstarch

2 teaspoons xanthan gum

1 teaspoon baking powder

½ teaspoon baking soda

1 teaspoon cinnamon

½ cup cold non dairy margarine

½ cup packed brown sugar

1 teaspoon vanilla extract

⅓ cup non dairy milk

¼ cup agave

¼ cup molasses

3 tablespoons turbinado sugar mixed with

½ teaspoon cinnamon

- In a large bowl, whisk together the buckwheat flour, superfine brown rice flour, tapioca flour, cornstarch, xanthan gum, baking powder, baking soda, and cinnamon until thoroughly mixed.

- In a separate bowl, cream together the margarine and sugar until smooth. Mix in the vanilla extract, nondairy milk, agave, and molasses. Gradually add in the flour mixture until all are incorporated and continue to mix until a stiff dough is formed. Add a touch more buckwheat flour if it is sticky.

- Divide into two sections and pat into disks. Preheat oven to 350°F. Chill each disk briefly (about 15 minutes in freezer), and then roll out in between two pieces of parchment paper until a little less than ¼ inch thick. Cut into squares and poke holes in the top (I used the tip of a chopstick) to poke holes and also to perforate the cracker. For easy rolling and transferring, keep the dough cold. If it starts to lose shape easily, pop it back in the freezer (still on the rolling parchment) for a few minutes, and then go back to shaping the crackers.

- The dough will be quite flexible and very easy to pull off the parchment. Use a flat metal spatula to help you if needed. Place onto an ungreased cookie sheet, sprinkle lightly with the mixture of turbinado and cinnamon, and bake in preheated oven for about 12 to 14 minutes, or until firm and a touch darker on edges.

- Let cool completely. Store in airtight container for up to 1 week.

# RUGELACH

My mother knows how to make some killer rugelach. While it's a traditional Jewish pastry that is enjoyed year-round, the cookies' fragrant fruit filling and crispy pastry crunch always marked the start of the holiday season in our house.

¼ cup soft dried apricots

½ cup dates, not too soft

1¼ cups walnuts

½ teaspoon cinnamon

¼ teaspoon nutmeg

¼ teaspoon salt

¼ cup sugar

1 to 1½ tablespoons apricot or strawberry jam

1 recipe Puff Pastry

- Preheat oven to 400°F. Place the apricots, dates, walnuts, cinnamon, nutmeg, salt, and sugar into a food processor and pulse until well combined. Add in the jam, 1 tablespoon at a time until the mixture clumps together.

- Roll out one-half of the puff pastry in between two sheets of parchment paper into a 12-inch circle. Using a pizza cutter, cut about ten even triangles. Place a small ball of the filling at the small tip of the triangle. Beginning at the opposite side, roll dough up to cover, sealing the tip when the filling is all bundled up. Repeat with the other half of the dough. Place the cookies onto an ungreased cookie sheet on the middle rack of the oven, about 1 inch apart, and bake for 20 minutes, or until golden brown. Store in airtight container for up to 2 weeks.

# CRISPY GLAZED LIME COOKIES

**YIELD: ABOUT 12 COOKIES**

These zingy cookies are delicious on their own and make an exceptional treat served with a scoop of Strawberry Ice Cream. Or, cut them slightly larger, then stuff with your favorite ice cream and freeze for an irresistibly sweet and tangy treat.

## COOKIES

¾ cup cold shortening

⅓ cup powdered confectioners sugar

¼ cup sugar

Zest of 1 lime (about 1 teaspoon)

2 tablespoons lime juice

½ teaspoon salt

1¼ cups sorghum flour

½ cup arrowroot starch

¼ cup tapioca flour

1 teaspoon xanthan gum

## GLAZE

1 cup confectioners sugar

5 tablespoons freshly squeezed lime juice

Lime zest to garnish

- Cream together the shortening, sugars, lime zest, and lime juice until smooth. In a separate bowl, whisk together the salt, sorghum flour, arrowroot starch, tapioca flour, and xanthan gum and then gradually incorporate into the sugar mixture while mixing just until a firm dough is formed. Flatten into a disk and chill in the freezer for about 15 minutes. While the dough chills, preheat oven to 350°F.

- Roll out dough in between two sheets of plastic cling wrap onto a flat surface until about ¼ inch thick. Cut into 2-inch squares and place onto an ungreased cookie sheet.

- Bake for 15 minutes. Let cool and add glaze to the tops. To make the glaze, simply whisk together the glaze ingredients until completely smooth and runny. Spoon onto the tops of the cookies and let dry about 10 minutes. Spoon on another layer and top with lime zest. Let glaze completely harden before serving. Store in airtight container for up to 1 week.

# PALMIERS

YIELD: 18 COOKIES

These prim and proper cookies are sure to impress at your next gathering with friends. They are so elegant and gorgeous, you won't believe how easy they are if you already have puff pastry on hand.

1  recipe <u>Puff Pastry</u>

1 cup turbinado sugar

1 tablespoon cornstarch mixed with 3 tablespoons water

* parchment paper.

* Divide the puff pastry in two sections and roll each out into two rectangles, about 12 inches by 6 inches. Dust the tops of each rectangle with ½ cup turbinado sugar to evenly cover. Starting from the edges of the two longest sides of the rectangle, roll the edges of the cookie inward, rolling two separate coils so that they face each other and eventually meet. You will have a long tube with two distinct sections. Cut into ½-inch-wide cookies and place directly onto the prepared cookie sheet. Brush with cornstarch mixture. Sprinkle with additional turbinado. Bake for 12 minutes, or until golden brown. Let cool completely before serving. Store in airtight container for up to 1 week.

# LAVENDER ICEBOX COOKIES

**YIELD: ABOUT 30 COOKIES**

Fresh lavender buds are best for these, but, if you don't have fresh, dried will certainly do. You can source dried lavender either online or in specialty herb stores; look for buds that have a nice deep lavender color on the tips. I like to place dried buds in an airtight glass container with an orange or lemon peel for about 1 hour before using to soften them up a bit.

1¼ cups sorghum flour

½ cup brown rice flour (superfine is best, but either can be used)

½ cup potato starch

¼ cup tapioca flour

1⅓ cups confectioners sugar

1 teaspoon xanthan gum

1 cup very cold non dairy margarine

1 tablespoon flaxseed meal

2 tablespoons water

½ cup granulated sugar for rolling

3 tablespoons fresh or dried lavender buds for rolling

* In a food processor, combine all the ingredients up through the xanthan gum and pulse several times to combine thoroughly. Add in the

margarine, about a tablespoon at a time, and continue to pulse until crumbly. In a small bowl, combine flaxseed meal with water and let rest until gelled, for about 5 minutes. Add in the prepared flaxseed meal and mix well until a tacky dough forms.

- Divide dough into two sections and shape each as best you can into a log using two pieces of parchment paper. To make perfectly round logs, freeze each log for about an hour, then roll (while still in the parchment) onto a flat surface to create a more even cylinder. Return to freezer and chill at least an additional hour and up to overnight.

- Once ready to bake, preheat oven to 350°F and spread another piece of parchment or foil with a mixture of the granulated sugar and lavender. On a flat surface, roll the log gently but firmly into the mixture to coat, making sure not to be too rough to break the dough. Slice using a sharp knife into ½-inch-thick rounds and place onto an ungreased cookie sheet.

Bake for 15 to 17 minutes, or until puffy and bottoms are light golden brown. Let cool completely before eating. Store baked cookies in airtight container for up to 1 week.

# MOCHA CRUNCHERS

**YIELD: 36 COOKIES**

Espresso and chocolate meet for a dark and delightful cookie that is easy to roll out and even easier to indulge in! These cookies freeze well both as a dough or prebaked. Simply thaw at room temperature for 30 minutes before baking or enjoying.


2 tablespoons flaxseed meal

¼ cup water

⅔ cup non hydrogenated shortening

1 cup sugar

1 teaspoon baking soda

1 teaspoon salt

1 teaspoon xanthan gum

1¼ cups brown rice flour

⅓ cup cocoa powder

½ cup teff flour

½ cup tapioca flour

2 teaspoons instant espresso powder

1 tablespoon non dairy milk

⅓ cup non dairy chocolate chips


* Preheat oven to 375°F. In a small bowl, mix the flaxseed meal with the water and allow to rest until gelled, for about 5 minutes.

- In a large mixing bowl, cream together the shortening and sugar along with the prepared flaxseed meal. Mix until smooth.

- In a separate bowl, whisk together the baking soda, salt, xanthan gum, brown rice flour, cocoa powder, teff flour, tapioca flour, and instant espresso powder. Bring together the shortening mixture and flour mixture until a crumbly dough forms and, while still mixing, add in the 1 tablespoon non dairy milk until the dough comes together. Form into two even disks and roll out in between two sheets of parchment paper until ¼ inch thick. Cut out using a cookie cutter and transfer to an ungreased cookie sheet using a flat metal spatula. Bake for 9 minutes. Remove from the oven and sprinkle chocolate chips over the hot cookies. Let set for 1 minute and then spread chocolate thinly over the tops of the cookies. Let cool completely before serving. Store in airtight container for up to 1 week.

# MATCHA COOKIES

**YIELD: 24 COOKIES**

Matcha is the powder of finely milled green tea leaves, most often used as a ceremonial tea. Seek out the highest-quality matcha you can for the best flavor. Matcha can be sourced from tea shops, online, and in many grocery chains that offer specialty items, such as Whole Foods.

1 tablespoon flaxseed meal

2 tablespoons water

¼ cup + 3 tablespoons non dairy margarine

⅓ cup confectioners sugar

2 tablespoons sugar

¾ cup sorghum flour

¼ cup tapioca flour

¼ cup potato starch

⅓ cup + 1 tablespoon almond meal

1 teaspoon xanthan gum

2 tablespoons matcha powder

- In a small bowl, mix together the flaxseed meal and water and let rest until gelled, for about 5 minutes.

- In a separate bowl, cream together the margarine and sugars until smooth. Add in the prepared flaxseed meal.

- In another bowl, whisk together the flours, potato starch, almond meal, xanthan gum, and matcha powder and then combine with the margarine mixture to form a soft, but workable dough. If the dough is too sticky, add a touch more sorghum flour until easy to handle. Wrap in plastic wrap and chill in freezer for about 15 minutes. While the dough chills, preheat oven to 350°F and line a cookie sheet with parchment paper or a silicone mat.

- Roll out the chilled dough to a thickness of ¼ inch in between two sheets of parchment paper. Remove top piece of parchment and cut into desired shapes using cookie cutters. Slide the bottom piece of parchment and the cookies onto a cookie sheet and chill for an additional 5 minutes in the freezer, or 15 minutes in the fridge. Using a flat metal spatula, carefully transfer the cut cookies to a parchment-covered baking sheet. Sprinkle with sugar and bake for 12 minutes. Let cool completely before serving. Store in airtight container for up to 1 week.

Have a matcha latte while the cookies bake! To make a simple latte, simply add 1 teaspoon matcha powder to 1 cup very hot non dairy milk. Froth with fork, add a touch of stevia or agave to taste. Voilà! Matcha bliss.

# LADYFINGERS

**YIELD: ABOUT 36 LADYFINGERS**

Use these as the base for Tiramisu or eat alone. When mixing, be sure to measure exactly as even a little too much liquid can cause these cookies, which are chickpea-based, to spread and become flatter than desired. If you have one available, a nonstick, lightly greased ladyfinger pan comes in handy for baking perfect ladyfingers.

½ cup brown rice flour

½ cup + 3 tablespoons besan/chickpea flour

2 tablespoons tapioca flour

2 tablespoons potato starch

2½ teaspoons baking powder

¼ teaspoon salt

½ teaspoon xanthan gum

¾ cup sugar

1 teaspoon apple cider vinegar

½ cup non dairy margarine, softened

⅔ cup non dairy milk

* Preheat oven to 375°F. Lightly spray a ladyfinger pan with a nonstick cooking spray or line a heavy cookie tray with parchment.

123

- In a large bowl, whisk together the dry ingredients until well mixed. Add the vinegar, margarine, and nondairy milk and mix vigorously until fluffy. Place into a piping bag fitted with a wide round tip and pipe about 1 tablespoon batter into the ladyfinger pan template or in a straight line, about 2 inches apart, straight onto the parchment paper. Be careful not to pipe too much batter or the cookies will spread.

- Bake for 13 to 15 minutes, or until golden brown on edges. Let cool completely before serving. Store in airtight container for up to 1 week.

# MADELEINES

**YIELD: 24 COOKIES**

These light and crisp cookies are perfect any time you want a treat but want to avoid anything that's overly heavy or dense. You'll want to pick up a madeleine pan or two to make these, but these can easily be sourced for under $10 at most kitchen supply stores or online.

3 teaspoons baking powder

¼ teaspoon salt

½ cup white rice flour

½ cup + 2 tablespoons besan/chickpea flour

2 tablespoons tapioca flour

3 tablespoons potato starch

½ teaspoon xanthan gum

1 cup confectioners sugar

1 teaspoon apple cider vinegar

½ cup non dairy margarine

½ cup non dairy milk

- Preheat oven to 375°F. Lightly spray a madeleine pan with a nonstick cooking spray or grease lightly with olive oil.

- In a large mixing bowl, whisk together the baking powder, salt, white rice flour, besan, tapioca flour, potato starch, and xanthan gum.

- Add the confectioner's sugar, apple cider vinegar, margarine, and nondairy milk and mix on high speed (or very fast using a sturdy balloon whisk) for 2

125

minutes using a whisk attachment until the batter is fluffy and smooth.

- Spoon about 2 teaspoons of batter into the madeleine molds and spread evenly using a small knife. The cookie molds should be three-quarters full. Rap the pan on an even surface a few times to remove any air pockets.

- Bake for 11 to 13 minutes, or until dark golden brown on seashell side and light blond on the bottoms. Let cool before gently removing from the molds. Store in airtight container for up to 1 week.

# HOLIDAY SPRITZ

**YIELD: 48 COOKIES**

These small, classic holiday cookies can be easy to make, but a little finesse is always appreciated. I recommend a metal cookie press over any others as the dough tends to stick less to them. Also, make sure the dough is chilled before piping for perfect results.

2 teaspoons egg replacer powder (such as Orgran)

2 tablespoons water

1½ cups brown rice flour

½ cup white rice flour

⅔ cup potato starch

1 teaspoon xanthan gum

1 cup non dairy margarine

1 cup confectioners sugar

1½ teaspoons vanilla extract

* In a small bowl, whisk together the egg replacer powder and the water. In a large bowl, whisk together the brown rice flour, white rice flour, potato starch, and xanthan gum. Cream together the margarine, sugar, and vanilla extract and then add the egg replacer mixture. Gradually add the flour mixture until a stiff dough forms. If dough seems too soft, add up to 2

127

tablespoons brown or white rice flour. Chill for 2 hours in refrigerator, until very cold.

- Preheat oven to 400°F.

- Place in cookie press and fit with disk of choice. Assemble press as instructed and press cookies into desired shapes onto a parchment-covered cookie sheet. Work quickly and be sure to keep the dough cold; this is key! Bake cookies for 7 minutes or until lightly golden brown on edges. Let cool completely before serving. Store in airtight container for up to 3 weeks.

# METRIC CONVERSIONS

The recipes in this book have not been tested with metric measurements, so some variations might occur.

Remember that the weight of dry ingredients varies according to the volume or density factor: 1 cup of flour weighs far less than 1 cup of sugar, and 1 tablespoon doesn't necessarily hold 3 teaspoons.

## General Formula for Metric Conversion

| | |
|---|---|
| **Ounces to grams** | multiply ounces by 28.35 |
| **Grams to ounces** | multiply ounces by 0.035 |
| **Pounds to grams** | multiply pounds by 453.5 |
| **Pounds to kilograms** | multiply pounds by 0.45 |
| **Cups to liters** | multiply cups by 0.24 |
| **Fahrenheit to Celsius** | subtract 32 from Fahrenheit temperature, multiply by 5, divide by 9 |
| **Celsius to Fahrenheit** | multiply Celsius temperature by 9, divide by 5, add 32 |

## Volume (Liquid) Measurements

1 teaspoon = ⅙ fluid ounce = 5 milliliters

1 tablespoon = ½ fluid ounce = 15 milliliters 2 tablespoons = 1 fluid ounce = 30 milliliters

¼ cup = 2 fluid ounces = 60 milliliters

⅓ cup = 2⅔ fluid ounces = 79 milliliters

½ cup = 4 fluid ounces = 118 milliliters

1 cup or ½ pint = 8 fluid ounces = 250 milliliters

2 cups or 1 pint = 16 fluid ounces = 500 milliliters

4 cups or 1 quart = 32 fluid ounces = 1,000 milliliters

1 gallon = 4 liters

## Oven Temperature Equivalents, Fahrenheit (F) and Celsius (C)

100°F = 38°C

200°F = 95°C

250°F = 120°C

300°F = 150°C

350°F = 180°C

400°F = 205°C

450°F = 230°C

# Volume (Dry) Measurements

¼ teaspoon = 1 milliliter

½ teaspoon = 2 milliliters

¾ teaspoon = 4 milliliters 1 teaspoon = 5 milliliters

1 tablespoon = 15 milliliters

¼ cup = 59 milliliters

⅓ cup = 79 milliliters

½ cup = 118 milliliters

⅔ cup = 158 milliliters

¾ cup = 177 milliliters 1 cup = 225 milliliters

4 cups or 1 quart = 1 liter

½ gallon = 2 liters 1 gallon = 4 liters

# Linear Measurements

½ in = 1½ cm

1 inch = 2½ cm

6 inches = 15 cm

8 inches = 20 cm

10 inches = 25 cm

12 inches = 30 cm

20 inches = 50 cm

CPSIA information can be obtained
at www.ICGtesting.com
Printed in the USA
BVHW091237040521
606415BV00004B/934